SILENCE AND PRAYER

A paper read at a Conference for Clergy in Winchester Diocese

MOTHER MARY CLARE, S.L.G.

S.L.G. PRESS

Convent of the Incarnation

Fairacres, Oxford

Seventh Impression 1982

ISBN 0 7283 0043 5
ISSN 0307-1405

This age which by its very nature is a time of crisis, of revolution and of struggle, calls for the special searching and questioning which is the work of the christian in his silence, his meditation, his prayer; for he who prays searches not only his own heart but he plunges deep into the heart of the world in order to listen more intently to the deepest and most neglected voices that proceed from its inner depths. Thomas Merton

Our modern society, in the midst of which Thomas Merton lived and for the sake of which he gave himself to the life of prayer as a Christian solitary, is basically materialistic. People's worth is largely measured in terms of what they earn, and the value of their lives is assessed by their external activities. Many dread retirement or old age for the simple reason that the meaning of life for them is centred in externals, and once the possibility of activity is taken away, the *raison d'etre* of living is lost. Psychiatrists tell us that our mental hospitals are full because people have lost (or never achieved) a really balanced inner life; their capacity for fully mature and lasting personal relationships has never developed, so life is purposeless for them and lacks clear directive.

The choice we Christians have to make is not between the importance of God and the importance of man, for where there is no knowledge of God or belief in God there can be no true understanding of the value and dignity of man. The Christian, in choosing to place God at the centre of his life, comes to see all human life and purpose as having eternal meaning in relation to God. The Christian is the true humanist.

Baron von Hugel expresses a tradition that goes back to Origen when he says, 'Man is what he does with his silence'. There is a terror in silence if one is only conscious of being an isolated individual, because man is made for fellowship, to be part of a family. Although speech is a necessary means of communication, there is a whole realm of human—as well as spiritual—exploration in which silence can be the medium of a positive exchange of communication. We are rapidly becoming unaware of this. We are afraid to be silent. Why? For one thing, in silence there is not the same opportunity for our own egoism— the false 'I'—to cover up a frightening emptiness. In our activity, even our altruistic activity, our aggressive, self-determinative, power-loving ego is unconsciously projected on to others, either to protect ourselves or to express ourselves.

If, however, we have any sense of communication with others in silence, it is God who is the link and not something we ourselves are doing or saying. That is why silence is so precious, so powerful. I am, of course, not referring merely to refraining from speech, but to a relaxed creative silence which is a medium for spiritual affinity and unity, a union of spirits in the one aim of seeking God and seeking each other in God. We can see how important the positive use of silence should be to each one of us in our life of prayer.

Silence is the matrix of eternity, a truth expressed in the well-known words of a hymn by the Quaker poet, John Greenleaf Whittier:

> The silence of eternity
> Interpreted by love!

In the Gospels we see how our Lord took his over-taxed disciples apart to rest in a form of prayerful withdrawal after their busy days of active ministry. We also see that he himself found communion with the Father in the silence of his night prayer.

The Fathers of the Church, both Eastern and Western, and especially Cassian—the great exponent of desert spirituality—identified this silence with charity and purity of heart 'since it consists in always offering to God a most pure heart . . . untouched by all perturbations'. In such silence we are not content with exorcising noise: we submit body and soul to the rhythm of the Spirit. Silence, which is not just absence of speech, is shown to be synonymous with loss of self, with a stillness of spirit in which the true self—which God made in his own image and likeness—may be released from the shackles of fear in which we imprison it and we may know by experience the splendour of the liberty of the children of God: God dwelling in us and we in him.

From such listening silence in our prayer there must come a stilling of the mind, a cessation of the ceaseless chatter to ourselves about the memories which surge up from the unconscious and which ruin for many of us our time of prayer by driving out any sense of simple quiet attention to God. Many people are disturbed by the fact that times of prayer may be times of genuine temptation of psychological and even sexual fantasies, but this need not disturb us. It is to be expected that those lower levels, which we can keep at bay by activity, should come to the surface when we try to be still before God. There they can be faced and acknowledged in positive penitence and redirected as needed into deeper penitence and more simple dependence on the Holy Spirit's action.

In prayer, as in life, the cleansing of the memory and the stilling of an over-active imagination is an integral part of the purgative way. We must remember that suppression is dangerous and can be the cause of spiritual accidie as well as psychological disturbance, but the cleansing that unifies and stills us must come through the uprising of love, the desire to be wholly God's. True silence is to be found in the willingness to be wholly conformed to God's will. As Gilbert Shaw expressed it in his book, *The Face of Love:*

> Look well, O soul, upon thyself
>   lest spiritual ambition
>   should mislead and blind thee
>   to thy essential task:
>   to wait in quietness,
>   to knock and persevere in humble faith.

Knock thou in love, nor fail to keep thy place before the door
    that when Christ wills—and not before—
    he shall open unto thee the treasures of his love.

Grant me humility of soul
    that I may grow in penitence
    dependent on the Holy Spirit's light.

The silence from speech, the stilling of the memory, imagination, and mind must ultimately lead to that conformity of will wherein God will ask nothing less than everything and in which our prayer can be but an echo of the prayer in the garden of Gethsemane: 'Thy will be done'.

What this dimension of silence means in relation to our prayer is an intensely personal matter, but in order that prayer may become a dialogue of love, a unity of the human heart with God, we need to rest more on the activity of the Holy Spirit. As Mother Teresa of Calcutta said to Malcolm Muggeridge:

> We need to find God and he cannot be found in noise and restlessness. God is the friend of silence. Is not our mission to give God to others, not a dead God but a living God? The more we receive in silent prayer, the . . . more we can give. . . . We need silence to be able to touch souls. The essential thing is not what we say, but what God says through us. (*Something Beautiful for God.*)

It is in a silence of waiting and expectancy that God speaks through us. In Mother Teresa and her Sisters—in their work with starving, dying, abandoned men, women, and children—we see an example of persons in whom the false self has been burnt away by the love of Christ and in whom contemplation and activity are completely united. We have not all reached that unity of the true self in God, but at least we can recognize in ourselves our need for that emptiness of self which God may fill, substituting his love and his will for our self-chosen activities.

4

We can recognize our need for times of withdrawal and quiet, when we can be still and let God fill us with himself. It is in that stillness that the vision is given 'without which the people perish', the vision which the Church so badly needs if it is to be truly renewed. In the reality of the silence of the heart, those nourished by the teaching of Christ can and do understand and communicate with each other wordlessly. This silence is the source of the prophetic power possessed by men and women of vision. This, in part, is why many today are seeking a form of deeper withdrawal in the recovery of the eremitical life.

When we first enter upon the way of silence, the mere lack of noise may be more disturbing than the continuous noise of our neighbour's radio or the roaring of jet planes overhead, for in the exterior silence we find that *inner* noise cuts across the attention we desire to give to God. We need not worry about this but when we become aware of it, should return gently to the still centre of our being where God is at work imperceptibly but surely. As Thomas Merton taught, silence is the condition of prayer and the doorway into the cosmic need of the world, the condition of that profound prayer which cries out from the heart of the universe because it expresses the love of Christ, crucified and risen, for the world.

Such profound prayer, however, is not concerned only with the cosmos as a whole, but also with the most mundane details of our very ordinary, everyday lives, for, as Henri le Saux, O.S.B. writes in his book *Prayer*:

Prayer is not a part-time occupation for any of Christ's disciples, nor indeed is it so for any truly religious man. There are no part-time contemplatives, any more than there are part-time Christians or part-time men. To live in the presence of God should be as natural for a Christian as to breathe the air which surrounds him. To live in the presence of the Almighty is a birthright. It is the spontaneous expression of his love for the Lord when he knows that he is the child of God.

And Monica Furlong, in her book *Contemplating Now*, has as her basic premise that without the contemplative dimension in our lives we cannot be fully human. This contemplative dimension is the fruit of our willingness to meet the discipline of learning to wait in silence and stillness, as well as the boredom and loneliness and sometimes the apparent emptiness and barrenness which confront us in the waiting. This is the opinion of a free lance journalist who is also a busy housewife and mother. In the face of this opinion, it might be a chastening experience to ask ourselves whether we prefer to be constantly busy because it is so much easier and safer and more comfortable than giving ourselves seriously to the work of prayer. It is not that Monica Furlong glorifies contemplation at the expense of action, nor that she is speaking of a high-flown esoteric type of prayer, she is concerned to demonstrate that life is meant to be rhythmical and that both contemplation and action are necessary to basic stability. She writes:

> What I believe we need in this [Western, activistic] situation is not a sudden Easternising of ourselves, a wholesale selling out to gurus and fakirs, or even to contemplative prayer. The immediate need seems to be for something much more modest and down to earth, a simple recognition that we are *rhythmical* creatures, creatures who, obviously enough, need to follow bursts of strenuous activity with periods of rest and quietness; creatures who, less obviously (and this is where we touch upon deep fears), will have a natural tendency to follow periods of rest and quietness with periods of strenuous activity.

We need to recognize our real need to take regular times of quiet, and to be disciplined in generous self-giving in our activity.

> Drop thy still dews of quietness,
>   Till all our strivings cease:
> Take from our souls the strain and stress,
> And let our ordered lives confess
>   The beauty of thy peace. (Whittier.)

Christian contemplation

Interior peace is the fruit of Christ's overcoming and of the Holy Spirit's outpouring. This peace is the ground of Christian contemplation. 'To apprehend the point of intersection of the timeless with time', in the words of T. S. Eliot in the *Four Quartets*, is not a vague anticipation of that face to face confrontation with God which will come to us all at the moment of our death. Contemplation, in the Christian sense, is living in the *now* of daily life in preparation for that moment of truth; it is living in the realization of God's love and his claim upon us. Indeed, any experience of the reality of God rests upon the belief that we *can* love him because, in the first instance, his love has created us, redeemed us, and—through the action of the Holy Spirit—is continually re-creating us and renewing in us the latent potentiality of union with himself, that union which is the end of human life, the purpose for which every human being is created.

For the Christian, the end of man is union with God in love, and we are meant to know something of that love, of that relationship with God, in this present life, to know it by prayer and contemplation and in loving relationship one with another in God. As St. Paul tells us, we can only know 'in part', but we could know so much more than we do if we could face the cost of what a life lived in union with Christ demands, if we could open ourselves to the power of the Holy Spirit to enlarge and deepen those latent powers and potentialities that our human spirit possesses. After all, the Christian life is directed to a goal beyond all human expectations, a goal which can only be attained by strength far beyond our unaided human capacity. Therefore, I stress that contemplation is a gift to be received, to be prepared for, rather than something we can train ourselves to do. 'The Holy Spirit whom the Father will send in my name will teach you everything and will call to mind all that I have told you,' said Jesus. And St. Paul said, 'Bear fruit in active goodness of every kind and grow in the knowledge of God so that Christ may present us before himself as dedicated men.' Christian contemplation is incarnational, not a negative journey

7

inwards, but the growth of unity of life and prayer, an increase in the knowledge of God shown forth by the wholeness of a consecrated life.

'Vacete et videte quoniam ego sum deus': 'Empty yourself and know that I am God.' The old Latin is so much stronger than the Authorised translation, 'Be still and know that I am God', for if we are truly empty, and then offer the ground of our soul and our natural intelligence and faculties to wait upon God in the desire of love, we *shall* grow in the way of naked faith, hope, and love, the way which is not dependent upon conscious realization or emotional experience. Christian prayer must never be seen as an excursion into transcendental experience, or as an escape from reality into a world of self-contemplation, but as receiving, quietly and often hiddenly, a knowledge of God wherein life becomes meaningful and unified. In Christian prayer the frequent sense of tension between contemplation and action is resolved, for both are recognized as aspects of the one great power of God's love poured into our hearts by the Holy Spirit who is Love.

Is this a dividing line between the Christian and the non-Christian way of life? Whereas all human beings must follow their reason and their conscience, informed by all the truth available to them, the Christian must follow the way of God as revealed by Christ, the way of self-giving, of death, and—by the pure gift of God—of resurrection. The Christian, united to Christ, and empowered by the Holy Spirit, is able to obey completely the command of God to love God with the whole mind, the whole soul, the whole heart, the whole strength, and to love his neighbour as himself. In silence and contemplation the Christian opens himself to this unifying power of God. As Tennyson said: 'Our wills are ours we know not how; Our wills are ours to make them thine.'

In a broadcast talk, Archbishop Anthony Bloom quoted the following words of a German mystic: 'We are as great as God and he is as small as we are.' These words seem to me to interpret the whole essence of Christian faith and to underline the essential difference between Christianity and the other world-wide religions, namely, that in and through the Incarnation, eternity has come to dwell in the midst of time. Romano Guardini, a Roman Catholic theologian, reminds us in one of his books that this same limitless and indefinable God stoops to become as small as our finite hearts, stretching them far beyond their natural capacity so as to enable us to share in his own infinitude. As Dame Julian of Norwich expressed it, 'We are all in him enclosed.'

In his book on Eastern Christian worship, *The Joy of Freedom*, Father Verghese of the Syrian Orthodox Church writes, 'God's transcendence is not a matter of the limits of our mind, He cannot be classified or located . . . he is not a God who fills the gaps in our thinking, he simply puts our thinking into its place. He cannot be thought about, he can only be worshipped in humble, loving, self-dedication. Modern man does not fully become human until he learns to worship his transcendent God.' And that is what prayer is all about. Man cannot be his true self unless he prays; without prayer he shrivels and becomes a pathetic caricature of his full potential.

J. B. Phillips gave one of his books the title, *Your God is too Small.* We are continually reducing God's stature by substituting ourselves as the measure by which we judge whether we are fully mature and fulfilled as human beings. If spirituality may be defined as the search for personal relationship between God and mankind, then spirituality is something being manifested in and through the present generation; it is not something out of the past, but something which embraces the whole of man's life in the present. Independently of God, man cannot understand either himself or his environment, hence his misuse of his creativity; his interior conflict and disharmony; his failure in personal relationships; his despair covered up by activism, pleasure seeking, and misguided efforts of self-realization. There also follows—and this is very important—his misuse of his natural environment, that misuse which has created the present world-wide problems of pollution. Man needs to approach spirituality with this sense of alienation from his true self and his true destiny and place in the scheme of things. In a return to genuine dependence on God—the acknowledgement of his status as a son of God in union with Christ—lies the only way to man's true maturity. In this spirituality of dependence on God, lies the way towards that reconciliation and unity at all levels of life for which the world is crying out. We need to realize the supremacy of the God who works through history, the God who is at work in the present moment of history, to heal the tensions and dichotomies of national life, church life, and individual life. The tensions of our day are legion; we will look at a few of the most crucial ones.

The tension between spirit and matter

Most religious and political philosophies today leave either the body or the spirit out of their reckoning, or else divide the two. Dialectical materialism, for example, ignores the spirit. Those who use drugs to induce mystical states seek to go out from the body. Many non-Christian, and even some Christian, sects regard the body as evil and as an obstacle to the life of the spirit.

Therefore, Christian spirituality has to be seen to be fully incarnational and sacramental. Christians should be a living witness to this fact, that Christianity is not esoteric but in a sense very 'ordinary'. The world should see the 'extra-ordinariness' of Christianity in the family love, the sacrifice, the obedience, the mutuality made incarnate in the Christian community, in its way of personal relationships, and its way of dealing with things. Christian spirituality affirms that the 'thing done in the body' is a true expression of the 'thing believed in the soul' and that both the act and the belief have eternal value.

The tension between freedom and determinism

Psychology, medicine, science, some religions and sects minimize man's moral responsibility, regarding him as the slave of physical and psychical forces rather than as a free agent.

In the face of this, Christian spirituality stresses judgment, mercy, and redemption. It does not deny the discoveries which affirm the diminished responsibility of the individual for what he does in many instances, but it denies that this is the last word. Christ descends into the unconscious, and he ascends beyond our earthly conceiving. Christians must witness to the world the power of the total Christ to heal and change lives. The 'slave of Christ' is a free man, witnessing the power of Christ amid natural causes and disabilities in his life and his prayer. Not death, but the resurrection of the body and the transfiguration of the cosmos is the end, the goal, of human life.

The tension between thought and action

This is the basic division between the contemplative East and the activist West; it is also a division which is present in every soul and in every church. It is, however, a division which I believe can be bridged by the right understanding of Christian contemplative prayer.

The positive answer to these tensions lies, surely, in the increasing realization of present day Christians of the equal value and the rich uniqueness of each individual vocation within the total Body of Christ, and this points the way to a truer realization of the Church's vocation as a whole, to the unity in diversity of races, churches, and particular traditions, to the realization that it is not even desirable that we should all be the same. Within the one Christ there is great diversity of vocation. But prayer in Christ—in its manifold forms—is the birthright of all Christian people. It is the fruit of our initiation by baptism and the Spirit into the Body of Christ. Prayer is, thus, not a self-activated process but a release of God's own energy, the work of the Holy Spirit in us.

> . . . the Spirit comes to the aid or our weakness. We do not even know how we ought to pray, but through our inarticulate groans the Spirit himself is pleading for us, and God who searches our inmost being knows what the Spirit means, because he pleads for God's own people in God's own way; and in everything, as we know, he co-operates for good with those who love God and are called according to his purpose. (Romans 8:26-28, *N.E.B.*)

11

But we must not take this gift lightly or expect the Spirit to act magically: prayer, like the Sacraments, requires our personal co-operation and response to the Spirit. The ability to pray, to enter into communion with God, is a gift of God, an expression of his love for man, but a gift that calls for a freely-willed reception on man's part. Each person must decide whether he is willing to pay the cost of entering into a continually renewed and continually deepening relationship with God in prayer. In this connection, we may well recall some words of Father Figgis, C.R. in the Hulsean Lectures delivered before the University of Cambridge in 1908:

> It is not to pleasant days and well fashioned lives and sheltered peace that Christ summons you, but to tears and the splendour of sacrifice, and the height and depth of lives lived in warfare, a world of wonder and joy, but of anguish and agony.

These words were spoken to a generation largely wiped out by World War I, but in their application today they demand the same spirit of sacrifice of each one of us in our Christian commitment. Let us consider, then, what prayer really asks of us, prayer which is not a part-time occupation but the expression of our complete dedication to God.

Dispositions for prayer

Prayer, if it is worthy of the name, implies total commitment, and total commitment asks of us a true and costing *metanoia*. As a man sows so shall he reap, and as a man lives, so shall he pray. Prayer and life, living and praying, are indivisible. In order that contemplative prayer may truly be the bringing of the Holy Spirit into the world's pain and tensions, there must be an element of costly purification, of positive detachment for those giving themselves seriously to the work of prayer. If prayer is learning to unite our will with the will of God, then the cost must be the cost of Calvary. To learn to love as Christ loves is to discover through *metanoia* the true renewing of our whole being, in God, on behalf of the world. This, surely, is another essential mark of Christian contemplation, that it is inseparable from Christ's way of reconciliation which is the true context of intercession.

To learn to love as Christ loves involves both *theoria*, vision, and spiritual conflict. To let our love, our desire, our faculties, be taken and transformed by Christ in the Spirit, is to discover the power of *metanoia*, the *renewing of our whole being before God. Theoria* is a turning to God, turning away from the world for the sake of the world, turning to God that our feebleness may be healed, purified by his strong holiness so that a little of his glory may be reflected in us. There can be no substitute for the deepened life of prayer and communion with God, communion with God which implies both death and resurrection, an entering into the darkness of contemplation which no tongue can explain. So T. S. Eliot writes:

> You must go by a way wherein is no ecstasy.
> In order to arrive at what you do not know,
> You must go by a way which is the way of ignorance.
> In order to possess what you do not possess
> You must go by the way of dispossession.
> In order to arrive at what you are not
> You must go through the way in which you are not.
> And what you do not know is the only thing you know
> And what you own is what you do not own
> And where you are is where you are not.

The practice of prayer

Archbishop Temple once said, 'We must learn to pray as we are and not as we are not.' In other words, there are as many ways of the soul's approach to God as there are different personalities. Each must find his own particular way, but is there a common practice for us all? I do not hesitate to say that the common practice for us all is our knowledge of and our praying of the Bible.

In the great tradition of Christian prayer, whether it be that of the desert Fathers or the later centuries of monastic practice in both East and West, the Bible has always been the ground of true prayer. In the West, later medieval and post-Tridentine spirituality built up more intellectual systems of prayer which many Christians today do not find helpful. Our danger in rejecting these systems is that we will drift into a vague, formless 'prayer' which is all too often and too loosely called 'contemplative'. Christian prayer must never be confused with 'transcendental meditation' or 'mystical experience' induced by L.S.D. or any other form of esoteric experience.

The desert Fathers were content to repeat over and over again such affirmations of trust and dependency on God as, 'O God make speed to save me: O Lord make haste to help me', which we in the West took over as the opening of our daily office. St. Benedict taught his monks to make their prayer short and simple, based on the recitation of the Psalms and a simple brooding on the words of the Scriptures, memorising or reciting a verse or portion of the Bible till their mind was stilled and their heart warmed by the constant intaking of divine truth, so that their will was moved to be conformed to the will of God. Let us remember that their reading of Scripture was carried out in great simplicity, without the aid of commentaries. This, I think, tends to make this way of prayer difficult for us to grasp today, though it is, none the less, a necessary way, for priests, theologians, ordinands, teachers, and all lay people. Without this way of prayer, the priest's daily recitation of the Office, for example, can become a mechanical duty rather than the open door to a growing intimacy with God.

'In the scriptures, with faces unveiled, we shall behold the glory of the Lord,' said Origen. In the simple desert prayer, Scripture was read slowly and meditatively: a ruminating on the words, which were pronounced with the lips as well as read by the eyes. This entrance of the words by means of both ears and eyes meant that they were planted deep in the very being of the reader. This has been described as 'the conceiving of the Word in the heart'.

It is a primary condition of hearing the Word that the mind be free and alert, and the heart clean and open. In this condition the Holy Spirit can bring home to the soul the message God wants it to receive, not only the literal facts or thoughts, but their existential realization in the life of the reader, its fruit-bearing in his words and actions. By listening to the Word and allowing it full play in our hearts we find ourselves moved to respond, and true prayer is born, the brooding prayer of one who converses with the Lord and answers his call.

The effect of this brooding and communing with God is expressed by Origen in his Homily on Psalm 36: 'Then the word of God shall have come into your souls and clinging to your hearts will form your minds according to the image of the word itself, i.e. that you should desire and do what the word of God wills, and thereby Christ himself will be formed in you.'

In this connection, consider the passage in Exodus 33 where the writer speaks of the Tent of Meeting 'pitched without the camp' and 'afar off from it', placed, that is, in solitude and silence, away from the noise and bustle of the camp. As Moses enters the Tent, the pillar of cloud descends, the sign and symbol of the Presence of God, the God who had revealed himself to Moses at Horeb, and whom Moses had worshipped and obeyed. Then there follows, 'And the Lord spoke unto Moses face to face, as a man speaketh unto his friend.'

In like manner we, as seekers after God, find that God gives himself to us abundantly. He first reveals himself, and if we respond in worship and obedience, if we wait upon him in silence and solitude, we enter into true communion, true conversation with him. There is question and answer, command and obedient reply, a dialogue of mutual giving and receiving. This gives us a clue as to how to use our prayer time if it hangs heavy upon us, if we cannot concentrate, if we are sleepy or restless, if we do not know what to say. Do we give God a chance to speak? He is the prevenient God who takes the initiative. Our dumbness and inability to speak may be the result of not having listened to what he has to say to us. How much easier it is to enter into a conversation when someone asks us a question! Then we can reply. So in our relation with God, let us open our Bibles and read, slowly, prayerfully, and *wait*. Then, when God speaks to us through the words of the Bible, we will reply in true dialogue—perhaps sometimes to argue with God, as Abraham, Moses, and the prophets sometimes did—but ultimately to praise and thank him, and—possibly in silence rather than words—to love him and offer ourselves in obedience to him. So often, as St. Teresa said, 'We sit about like dolts, saying and doing nothing.' We must be alert, listening, responsive, open to receive the Word in our heart, and then to let it conceive and bear fruit.

It must be for each individual to determine personally what the practice of prayer means in terms of fidelity in setting aside time for prayer daily or weekly, and of perseverance in prayer when, as is inevitable, the practice seems unpalatable and meaningless. True prayer rests not in emotional experience but in steadfastness of the will set to will only what God desires. We must accept the fact that we shall never know the true meaning of prayer without perseverance in the act of praying itself.

While it is important to realize that our brooding prayer based on Scripture feeds and makes alive our eucharistic worship (and the recitation of the daily Office if we are committed to that), and likewise that liturgical prayer keeps our so-called 'private prayer' from becoming too subjective, I believe it is also one of the signs of the times that for many people, lay and ordained, the non-liturgical form of their prayer is becoming increasingly simple, still, wordless except for very short affirmations of praise, love, penitence. Even the repetition of a single word, such as the Holy Name of Jesus, or some ejaculation such as, 'O God, thou art my God', is sufficient to express the prayer of the heart. All the desire of the heart can be breathed out in the one word, 'God'.

Many today are turning to the Eastern Orthodox practice of the recitation of the Jesus Prayer: 'Jesus Christ, Son of the Living God, be merciful to me a sinner.' This prayer has the whole of theology in it, and its repetition is one good method of establishing the basis of our

16

prayer on a firm foundation. First, there is the statement of Jesus as the Christ, the Son of God. He is Lord and God, not just another good friend, another nice person to talk to, but God and Saviour. This concept of the majesty and judgment of God is important : it really is GOD whom we worship, and even if we 'put [our] hand in the hand of the man from Galilee', we find there God, who is heartbreak as well as joy, dread as well as peace, and judgment as well as mercy. We have to establish for ourselves clearly the plain fact of our state as creatures, as sinners, as servants before our Lord and our God.

Then, there is me, myself, the person who prays, who is alienated from God : 'a sinner', one who has fallen short of the glory of God and sees in the face of the Lord's majesty his own unworthiness. And in between these two—the majestic God and the sinner—there is *eleison*, 'mercy', the loving-kindness of our God. That is the basic theological fact that our whole life is to realize : God is in Christ reconciling the world unto himself in us and through us day by day; and *that* is the life of prayer.

In this life of prayer, this process of reorientation of ourselves towards God, we have to learn how to acknowledge that we are sinners; not by emotional self-depreciation, not by grudging psychoanalysis, but by looking towards God with hands empty and open to receive his mercy, to allow him to lead us on to the next thing he has in store for us. In prayer, that is, in true theology—living theology—repentance does not mean misery but genuine conversion of heart. It is the way of those often unpopular words : 'cross', 'crucifixion', 'asceticism', 'duty', and 'rule'. A fourteenth century English writer, quoting an older source, put it like this (and 'Order' may be referred to any way of life, although he referred to his own religious Order) :

Nailed and spread fast on my Rood in this holy Order,
as thou was nailed for me on thy hard rood :
here will I dwell with thee and never down from it come
until thou shalt bid me descend.

17

In conclusion I return to the opening quotation from Thomas Merton, to the thought that 'the work of the christian in his silence, his meditation, his prayer' is that of 'special searching and questioning' whereby 'he plunges deep into the heart of the world in order to listen more intently to the deepest and most neglected voices that proceed from its inner depths'. The whole theological point of what I have been saying in elaborating this thought is well summarized by these words written by Karl von Hase, the grandfather of Dietrich Bonhoeffer:

Everything has its time:
The Lord of time is God;
The turning point in time is Christ;
The right spirit of the times is the Holy Spirit.